PHILIPPINES

POSTAL ISSUES OF
THE JAPANESE OCCUPATION

Published in the United Kingdom in 2019 for Old Guard Press
by Shearsman Books Ltd
50 Westons Hill Road
Emersons Green
BRISTOL
BS16 7DF
to whom permissions enquiries should be directed

ISBN 978-1-84861-408-6

Copyright © Roderick Hall, 2019

The right of Roderick Hall to be identified as the author of this
work has been asserted by him in accordance with the
Copyrights, Designs and Patents Act of 1988.
All rights reserved.

PHILIPPINES

POSTAL ISSUES OF THE JAPANESE OCCUPATION

Including
Occupation Stamps as issued before the war
and
Liberation & Victory Commonwealth Stamps

COMPILED AND EDITED BY
Roderick Hall

ISSUED FEBRUARY 8 1959

Scott 650

Scott 651

INDEX

Acknowledgments	i
Introduction	ii
Postal Issues of the Japanese Occupation	1
Postal Rates	3
Postal Issues	4
Semi-Postal Issues	31
Postage Due	35
Official Issues	39
Appendix I	
Occupation Stamps as Issued Before the War	49
Appendix II	
Liberation - Hand-stamped Victory	59
Victory / Commonwealth	64

ACKNOWLEDGEMENTS

Warm thanks to Sebastian Baldassarre for his gift of a small booklet of Japanese occupation stamps, which kindled my curiosity to know more about these stamps. Nigel Gooding has an extensive knowledge of Philippine stamps, and has been very generous with his time and support on this project. My sincere thanks and warm appreciation for his help and friendship.

Thanks to Karen Hall, who spent many hours helping me design this booklet. Waldette Cueto and Lou Gopal provided a selection of photographs of the magnificent Manila Post Office. Lou's *Manila Nostalgia* online series is a precious window into pre-war Manila, once known as the Pearl of the Orient, as well as many other aspects of life in the Philippines. George Baker pointed out the subtle position of the flag in the Kalayan Independence issues, a keen observation.

Two books were extremely helpful: Eugene A Garrett's *A Postal History of the Japanese Occupation of the Philippines 1942-1945* and Peter W A Harradine's *Philippine Postage Stamp Handbook 1854-1982*. There is a wealth of knowledge in each book.

The International Philippine Philatelic Society's official publication, Philippine Philatelic News, is full of timely and interesting articles. Several articles dating back over 30 years provided useful information for Appendices I and II. I am proud to be a new member of the IPPS, the pre-eminent scholarly organisation for the study of Philippine postage stamps.

INTRODUCTION

This book started with a generous gift by Sebastian Baldassarre of Japanese occupation stamps to my collection on WWII at Filipinas Heritage Library. Many occupation stamps were based on pre-war Philippine stamps overprinted and surcharged in black by the Japanese Administration. I became curious to know how these stamps looked without the overprints. The more I delved, the more fascinating the subject became. Thus this booklet, limited to stamps issued by the Japanese Military Administration during the occupation of the Philippines, together with the same stamps as they appeared both before and after the occupation.

The booklet lists the stamps issued during the occupation by category and date of first issue except the first series designed and printed in Japan. Released on six occasions over a period of a year, they are grouped together. Second overprintings are listed under the original release date. Appendix I shows the stamps as issued under colonial and Commonwealth administrations during the 1930's. Appendix II shows stamps provisionally hand-stamped VICTORY issued in Leyte soon after the landings in October 1944 and the VICTORY - COMMONWEALTH stamps issued to celebrate the liberation. This book has required much detail. All errors and omissions are mine.

Most of the stamps in this booklet are fairly easy to acquire, except for those hand stamped VICTORY. These are hard to find and expensive as so few were hand stamped. Fortunately, good scans are available of all the overprinted stamps.

The Post Office building in Manila is a beautiful neoclassical building. Completed in 1930, it was destroyed in the battle for Manila, and has been rebuilt. I have taken the opportunity to fill blank pages between Sections of this booklet with photographs of the building and reproductions of Philippine stamps featuring the building.

There is no need to expand the brief descriptions of occupation stamps. We are fortunate to have *A Postal History of the Japanese Occupation of the Philippines, 1942-1945* by Eugene A Garrett, without doubt the definitive scholarly work on this subject. Privately printed in 1992, Library of Congress number 91-078196.

RH

ALL ISSUED SEPTEMBER 15 1967

65th Anniversary of the Bureau of Post
Jones Bridge and Pasig River in the forefront

Scott 973

Scott 974

Scott 975

POSTAL ISSUES
OF THE JAPANESE OCCUPATION

COMMENCEMENT OF THE POSTAL SERVICE UNDER THE JAPANESE OCCUPATION

The Japanese Army occupied Manila on January 2 1942, and the Commander-in-Chief of the Imperial Japanese Forces immediately activated the Japanese Military Administration with orders to efficiently bring the Philippines under Japanese Control and into the Greater East Asia Co-Prosperity Sphere.

On Wednesday March 4 1942, less than nine weeks after the occupation of Manila, postal service was resumed in that city. Over the following months service was extended across the regions.

First stamps released were the so-called Provisional or Emergency Issues, based on pre-war stamps approved by Japanese censors with the words 'United States of America' and 'Commonwealth' deleted in black. Several later issues were designed and printed in Japan. The occupation also marked the issuance of the first Philippine semi-postal stamps.

CHART OF POSTAL RATES DURING THE JAPANESE OCCUPATION

1. Domestic Mail

Effective Date	First Class		Second Class (b)	Third Class (c)	Registry Fee	Registered Letter	Registry Return Receipt
	Letters (a)	Cards					
Mar 4 1942	2c	2c	x	x	16c	18c	x
Sep 1 1942	5c	2c	1c	x	16c	21c	x
Dec 4 1942	(2c) (d)						
Dec 10 1942	5c	2c	1c	4c	16c	21c	x
Mar 1 1943	5c	2c	1c	4c	12c	17c	x
Mar 10 1943	5c	2c	1c	4c	12c	17c	5c
Dec 1 1943	(2c) (d)						
June 1 1944	5c	2c	1c	10c	20c	25c	5c

(a) Rate per each 20 grams or fraction thereof.
(b) Rate per 200 grams or fraction thereof, and 1c per each additional 100 grams or fraction thereof.
(c) Rate per each 100 grams or fraction thereof. Weight limited to four kilos to the general public, to ten kilos to government offices and to the Philippine National Bank and its branches.
(d) Special temporary rates for Christmas and New Year greeting cards, effective Dec 4-31 1942, and Dec 1-31 1943.

2. Foreign Mail

Rates for Foreign Mail were the same as those prevailing for Domestic Mail from the inauguration of Foreign Mail Service on October 5 1942, until May 14 1944. Effective May 15 1944, the following rates were ordered:

First Class		Second Class	Third Class)	Registry Fee	Registered Letter
Letters	Cards				
7c	3c	2c	6c	20c	27c

Japanese Occupation Stamps of the Philippines

PROVISIONAL OR EMERGENCY ISSUES

ISSUED MARCH 4 1942

Quantity 3,000,000   Scott N1
2-centavos apple green
Overprinted in black on
2-centavos Regular Issue of 1941
Jose Rizal

Quantity 160,000   Scott N3
16-centavos deep blue
Overprinted in black on
16-centavos Regular Issue of 1938
Magellan's Landing

These two were the first stamps surcharged and issued after the promulgation of the new postal regulation by the Japanese administration.

It is worth noting that soon after the issuance of the apple green 2c Jose Rizal, it was noticed that Rizal's hair part was on the wrong side of his head. This was corrected after the war with the issuance of the sepia 2c Jose Rizal, Scott 497, issued on May 28 1946 the last stamp issued before the independence of the Philippines.

Roderick Hall Collection
Filipinas Heritage Library

VICTORY ISSUE
FALL OF BATAAN AND CORREGIDOR

ISSUED MAY 18 1942

Quantity 100,000   Scott N8
2-centavos on 4-centavos green
Surcharged in black on 4-centavos Regular Issue of 1935
Allegory of Agriculture, Woman & Carabao

Issued to commemorate the fall of Bataan on April 9 1942 and the subsequent final surrender of the United States Army Forces in the Far East (USAFFE) to the Imperial Japanese Forces at Corregidor on May 6 1942.

The Filipino and American forces on Bataan surrendered on April 9 1942, ending organised opposition by the USAFFE to the Japanese forces on Luzon. Corregidor, the largest of four islands guarding the entrance to Manila Bay, with an extensive network of tunnels and formidable defensive positions, denied the Japanese the use of Manila Bay, the finest natural harbour in the Far East. After the landing of Japanese troops and two days of intensive fighting, Corregidor surrendered on May 6 1942. This defeat marked the fall of the Philippines, but the Japanese timetable for the conquest of Australia was severely set back.

PROVISIONAL REGULAR ISSUE

FIRST OVERPRINTING (THICK LONG TOP BAR)
ISSUED SEPTEMBER 1 1942
SECOND OVERPRINTING (THIN SHORT TOP BAR)
ISSUE DATE C EARLY 1943

Surcharged in black 5-centavos on 6-centavos Regular Issue of 1939
La Dalaga (Filipino Maiden)

Scott N4
Golden Brown

Scott N4a
Golden Brown

Scott N4b
Dark Brown

Scott N4c
Dark Brown

FIRST ANNIVERSARY
GREATER EAST ASIA WAR
ISSUED DECEMBER 8 1942

Quantity 400,000   Scott N9
Surcharged in black on 4-centavos Regular Issue of 1935
Allegory of Agriculture, Woman & Carabao

Issued to commemorate the First Anniversary of the Greater East Asia War.

The Japanese inscription is *Daitoa Senso/Isshunen Kinen* (Greater East Asia War/First Anniversary).

PROVISIONAL REGULAR ISSUE

ISSUED JANUARY 11 1943

Quantity 210,000   Scott N5
Surcharged in black 16-centavos on 30-centavos Regular Issue of 1939
Blood Compact

On March 16 1565, Miguel Lopez de Legaspi and Rajah Sikatuna of Bohol, sealed their friendship through a blood compact, considered the First Treaty of Friendship between two different races, religions, cultures and civilisations. It was a treaty of friendship based on respect and equality. The event is commonly known as *Sandugo*.

FIRST ANNIVERSARY

PHILIPPINE EXECUTIVE COMMISSION

ISSUED JANUARY 23 1943

Quantity 400,000   Scott N10
2-centavos on 8-centavos carmine

Quantity 200,000   Scott N11
5-centavos on 1-peso dull sepia

Surcharged in black on Air Mail stamps of 1941
Moro Vinta & Clipper

The katakana characters read Hito Giyo Seihu - Itu Nen Kinen
Philippine Executive Commission - First Anniversary

Commemorating the first anniversary of the Philippine Executive Commission, the puppet organisation created by the Japanese Military Administration to assist it in governing the country.

REGULAR ISSUES PRINTED IN JAPAN

The fourteen stamps of the Regular Issue that appear on the following pages were designed and printed in Japan and released gradually on six separate occasions over the period of a year, the first on April 1 1943, and the last on April 10 1944. These issues were used extensively throughout the islands.

There is conjecture that the amount of local detail in the stamps would indicate they were designed by unknown Filipino artists. The engravers are well known. The stamps were printed in Tokyo at the *Naikaku Insatsu Kyoku* (Cabinet Bureau of Printing).

The stamps are in four different designs:

Nipa Hut
1-centavo, 4-centavos, 20-centavos
Engraved by Matsuura, Masao

Girl Planting Rice
2-centavos, 6-centavos, 25-centavos
Engraved by Kato, Kurakichi

Mt Fuji & Mayon Volcano
5-centavos, 10-centavos, 21-centavos, 1-peso
Engraved by Noma, Kenichi

Moro Vinta
12-centavos, 16-centavos, 2-peso, 5-peso
Engraved by Watabe, Fumio

On the upper portion of the stamps, kanji was used: *Hito Yubin* (Philippine Postage), while katakana was used in the lower portion to denote the denominations of the stamps.

The monetary values in katakana at the bottom are *sentabo* (centavo) or *peso* (peso).

REGULAR ISSUES PRINTED IN JAPAN

ISSUED APRIL 1 1943

2-CENTAVOS REGULAR ISSUE

Quantity 10,400,000   Scott N13
2-centavos emerald green
Girl Planting Rice

5-CENTAVOS REGULAR ISSUE

Quantity 45,000,000   Scott N15
5-centavos orange brown shades
Mt Fuji & Mayon Volcano

Japanese Occupation Stamps of the Philippines

REGULAR ISSUES PRINTED IN JAPAN

ISSUED JUNE 7 1943

1 AND 4-CENTAVOS AND 1-PESO REGULAR ISSUE

Quantity 1,250,000   Scott N12
1-centavo orange vermillion
Nipa Hut

Quantity 1,300,000   Scott N14
4-centavos deep gray-green
Nipa Hut

Quantity 260,000   Scott N23
1-peso deep carmine
Mt Fuji & Mayon Volcano

Roderick Hall Collection
Filipinas Heritage Library

REGULAR ISSUES PRINTED IN JAPAN

ISSUED JULY 14 1943

6, 10, 12 AND 16-CENTAVOS REGULAR ISSUE

Quantity 520,000   Scott N16
6-centavos scarlet shades
Girl Planting Rice

Quantity 1,950,000   Scott N17
10-centavos turquoise
Mt Fuji & Mayon Volcano

Quantity 650,000
Less 350,000 surcharged December 8 1943
Scott N18
12-centavos steel blue
Moro Vinta

Quantity unknown   Scott N19
16-centavos sepia
Moro Vinta

REGULAR ISSUES PRINTED IN JAPAN

ISSUED AUGUST 16 1943

20, 21 AND 25-CENTAVOS REGULAR ISSUE

Quantity 650,000
Less 350,000 surcharged
December 8 1943
Scott N20
20-centavos rose violet
Nipa Hut

Quantity 750,000
Less 350,000 surcharged
December 8 1943
Scott N21
21-centavos violet
Mt Fuji & Mayon Volcano

Quantity 1,890,000   Scott N22
25-centavos pale brown shades
Girl Planting Rice

REGULAR ISSUES PRINTED IN JAPAN

2-PESO REGULAR ISSUE

FIRST PRINTING SEPTEMBER 16 1943
SECOND PRINTING APRIL 10 1944

Quantity first printing 40,000   Scott N24
Quantity second printing 55,000
2-peso dull violet
Moro Vinta

The entire issue of the 2-peso stamp was sold out before noon on the first day of issue. A second printing was issued on April 10 1944. The first printing had slightly heavier paper than the second printing and displays clear-cut perforations; the second printing frequently displays ragged perforations.

5-PESO REGULAR ISSUE

BOTH PRINTINGS ISSUED APRIL 10 1944

Quantity first printing 20,000   Scott N25
Quantity second printing 45,000
5-peso green
Moro Vinta

PROVISIONAL REGULAR ISSUE
KALIBAPI ISSUE
12-CENTAVOS REGULAR ISSUE
ISSUED APRIL 30 1943

Quantity 310,000   Scott N2
Surcharged in black on 12-centavos Regular Issue of 1940
12-centavos black
Salt Spring

The Salinas Salt Spring shown on the stamp is located in Pingkian, Nueva Ecija. The sketch of this issue was prepared by the Filipino painter Fernando Amorsolo for the 1938-40 Commonwealth issues. While considered as part of the *Kalibapi* issue, the design is not patriotic, and may have been issued as an expedient to fill the need for a 12-centavos Registry Stamp.

The three stamps of the *Kalibapi* are the last series of the provisional issues during the Japanese Occupation. This term is taken from *Kapisanan Sa Paglilingkod Sa Bagong Filipinas* (New Philippine Service Association). A special General Assembly of the *Kalibapi* ratified the Constitution of the so-called Philippine Republic on September 20 1943.

PROVISIONAL REGULAR ISSUE
KALIBAPI ISSUE
50-CENTAVOS REGULAR ISSUE
FIRST OVERPRINTING ISSUED APRIL 30 1943
SECOND OVERPRINTING ISSUED SEPTEMBER 7 1944

First Overprint Quantity 20,000 Second Overprint Quantity 125,000
Scott N6 Scott N6

Surcharged in black on 1-peso Regular Issue of 1938
50-centavos on 1-peso yellow and black, Barasoain Church

Seven stamps in the two printings have very minor variations that distinguish them from the other stamps in both overprintings.

In the first overprinting three irregularities occur on some sheets:

Position 3	C in CENTAVOS appears like an O
Position 8	5 and O of right 50 are connected
Position 11	V of CENTAVOS shaped like a Y

Four irregularities occur on the second overprinting:

Position 20	letters misaligned and misshapen in CENTAVOS
Position 21	right upstroke of N in CENTAVOS elongated at top
Position 22	misshapen O of CENTAVO
Position 25	elongated 5

Barasoan Church in Malolos, Bulacan, was where the Revolutionary Government drew up the constitution of the First (Aguinaldo) Philippine Republic on September 15 1893. The stamp was reissued on the first anniversary of Constitution Day of the Republika ng Pilipinas and only available at the Manila Central Post Office.

PROVISIONAL REGULAR ISSUE
KALIBAPI ISSUE
1-PESO REGULAR ISSUE
ISSUED APRIL 30 1943

Quantity 19,975   Scott N7
Surcharged in black l-peso on 4-peso Regular Issue of 1937
l-peso on 4-peso blue and black
Montalban Gorge

The mythical Bernardo Carpio, said to be trapped in Montalban Gorge by a talisman's power, is considered a saviour of Filipinos against national oppression. Revolutionary heroes Jose Rizal and Andres Bonifacio paid homage to the legend, the former by making a pilgrimage to Montalban, and the latter by making the caves of Montalban the secret meeting place for the Katipunan Movement, a revolutionary society founded in Manila in 1892, with the aim to gain independence from Spain through revolution.

FIRST ANNIVERSARY
FALL OF BATAAN AND CORREGIDOR
ISSUED MAY 7 1943

Quantity 1,000,000   Scott N26
2-centavos deep carmine red
Map of Manila Bay

Quantity 1,000,000   Scott N27
5-centavos deep emerald green
Map of Manila Bay

These stamps were designed by Yamanouchi Takao, Chief of the Small Design Section, Japanese Printing Bureau and Printed in Japan by photogravure on watermarked paper.

Translation of Katakana Syllabics

Top	*Firippin Yubin* (Philippine Postage)
Two lines below	*Bataan Korehidoru Kanraku Kinen/Isshunen Kinen* (Fall of Bataan-Corregidor/First Anniversary)
Bottom	*Showa juhachi nen gogatsu* (May 7 1943)
Under right-hand numeral	*Sentabo* (centavo)

LIMBAGAN ISSUE (PRINTING PRESS)
350th ANNIVERSARY OF THE PRINTING PRESS IN THE PHILIPPINES
ISSUED JUNE 20 1943

Quantity 350,000   Scott N28
Surcharged in black on 20-centavos Regular Issue of 1939
12-centavos on 20-centavos olive bistre
Juan de la Cruz

The first printing press in the Philippines was established by the Dominican friars in Manila in 1593, just twenty-eight years after the arrival of the Spaniards. Fray Juan Cobo is considered to have established the first press in the Philippines. This was built by Father Domingo de Nieva with the help of the Chinese printer Keng Yong. It was a simple xylographic press, where the woodblocks were carved, inked and the copy transferred onto paper. The first book is considered to be the *Doctrina Christiana*.

The woodcut cover page of *Doctrina Christiana* with Saint Dominic and the full title of the book.

Written by Fray Juan de Plasencia circa 1590, this is believed to be the first book printed in the Philippines.

ISSUED APRIL 1 1949

Scott B2

KALAYAAN (INDEPENDENCE) ISSUE

The issue consisted of three values: 5-centavos dull blue shades; 12-centavos red orange shade; 17-centavos bright carmine shades and a souvenir sheet. All values display the same design. *Kalayan Nang Pilipinas* translates as *Independence of the Philippines*. The inscription below is in the ancient Tagalan syllabary known as *Babayan*.

Japan granted independence to the Philippines on October 14 1943. Officials were elected by the people, under the control of the Central Japanese Government Authority. Jose P Laurel was elected President at the First Special National Assembly Session on September 25 1943 and inducted into office on October 14 1943. These stamps (designed by Guillermo E Tolentino, Filipino artist and sculptor) were issued to commemorate the event.

Usage as war ensign in *Kalayaan* issue, an interesting observation.

The Philippines does not utilise a separate war flag; instead, the national flag itself is used for this purpose. To indicate a state of war, the red field is flown upwards and is placed on the right (on the observer's left) if it is in a hanging position. In times of peace, however, the blue area is the superior field. This orientation of the flag was used during World War II, by both the Philippine Commonwealth from 1941 to 1945 and by the Japanese-sponsored Philippine Republic when it declared war against the United Kingdom and the United States in September 1944.

There is an anomaly in the use of the war flag in the *Kalayaan* stamp issue of October 14 1943, issued eleven months before the Japanese sponsored Philippine Republic declaration of a state of war. This observation made by George Baker suggests that this use of the flag and the fourth verse of Rizal's *Mi Ultimo Adios*, that appears on the souvenir sheet, could have been "...a subtle message of defiance against the Japanese Occupation, which only those acquainted with Philippine history would understand".

KALAYAAN (INDEPENDENCE) ISSUE
ISSUED OCTOBER 14 1943

Filipina at center, Rizal Monument at left, Filipino flag on pole at right, inner frame of broken chains and outer frame of pearls

Quantity Perf 750,000
Scott N29

Quantity Imperf 750,000
Scott N29a

Quantity Perf 650,000
Scott N30

Quantity Imperf 650,000
Scott N30a

Quantity Perf 500,000
Scott N31

Quantity Imperf 500,000
Scott N31a

SOUVENIR SHEET
KALAYAAN (INDEPENDENCE) ISSUE
ISSUED OCTOBER 14 1943

All stamps have the same design: Filipina at center; Rizal Monument at left; Filipino flag on pole at right; inner frame of broken chains and outer frame of pearls. Souvenir sheet contains the three stamps from the regular issue.

The Tagalog inscription at the top translates as:

Republic of the Philippines
Ministry of Public Works and Communications
Manila - 1943

The Tagalog inscription at the bottom translates:

Fourth stanza of *My Last Farewell* of Dr Jose Rizal

The inscription in cursive Spanish is a facsimile of the original manuscript of
Rizal's *Mi Ultimo Adios* (*My Last Farewell*)

Mis sueños cuando apenas muchacho adolescente,
Mis sueños cuando joven ya lleno de vigor,
Fueron el verte un día, joya del mar de oriente,
Secos los negros ojos, alta la tersa frente,
Sin ceño, sin arrugas, sin manchas de rubor.

My dreams, when scarcely a lad adolescent,
My dreams when already a youth, full of vigour to attain,
Were to see you, Gem of the Sea of the Orient,
Your dark eyes dry, smooth brow held to a high plane,
Without frown, without wrinkles and of shame without stain.

Japanese Occupation Stamps of the Philippines

SOUVENIR SHEET

Repúbliká ng Pilipinas
Kágawarán ng Gáwaing-Bayan at Páhatiran
Káwanihán ng Páhatiran
Maynilà—1943

Mis sueños cuando apenas muchacho adolescente,
Mis sueños cuando joven ya lleno de vigor,
Fueron el verte un día, joya del mar de oriente,
Secos los negros ojos, alta la tersa frente,
Sin ceño, sin arrugas, sin manchas de rubor.

(Ikaapat na talatà ng Hulíng Paalam ni Gat Jose Rizal)

Quantity 100,000   Scott NB4

Souvenir Sheet size is reduced by 20%

Roderick Hall Collection
Filipinas Heritage Library

SOUVENIR SHEET
NATIONAL HEROES
ISSUED FEBRUARY 9 1944
OFFICIALLY RE-RELEASED ON FEBRUARY 17 1944

Sheet of three values:

5-centavos blue
Jose Rizal

12-centavos carmine
Jose Burgos

17-centavos orange vermilion
Apolinario Mabini

Designed by Fernando Amorsolo

The day of issue marked the 107th birth anniversary of Dr Jose Burgos, a Filipino priest who championed the cause of native Filipino clergy. He was martyred during the Spanish Regime.

The Tagalog inscriptions at the top are:

Republic of the Philippines
Manila

and

By authority of Hon Quintin Paredes,
Minister of Public Works and Communications

Tagalog inscription at the bottom:

On the Birth of Nationalism in the Philippines

Japanese Occupation Stamps of the Philippines

SOUVENIR SHEET

REPUBLIKA NG PILIPINAS
MAYNILA

Sa kapahintulutan ng Kgg. QUINTIN PAREDES, *Kagawad ng mga Gawaing-Bayan at Pahatiran*

Sa pagsilang ng makabayang damdamin sa Pilipinas

Quantity 200,000   Scott NB8

Roderick Hall Collection
Filipinas Heritage Library

NATIONAL HEROES REGULAR ISSUE
ISSUED FEBRUARY 17 1944
PERFORATED

Quantity 500,000 | Quantity 300,000 | Quantity 200,000
Scott N32 | Scott N33 | Scott N34
5-centavos blue | 12-centavos carmine-red | 17-centavos red-orange
Jose Rizal | Jose Burgos | Apolinario Mabini

ISSUED APRIL 17 1944
IMPERFORATED

Quantity 200,000 | Quantity 200,000 | Quantity 200,000
Scott N32a | Scott N33a | Scott N34a
5-centavos blue | 12-centavos carmine-red | 17-centavos red-orange
Jose Rizal | Jose Burgos | Apolinario Mabini

These stamps commemorating the Philippine national heroes Jose Rizal, Jose Burgos and Apolinario Mabini, were patterned after the Famous American Series of 1940.

The day of issue, February 17 1944, was the 72nd anniversary of the 1872 execution by garrotting of three Filipino priests Fathers Jose Burgos, Mariano Gomez and Jacinto Zamora.

SECOND ANNIVERSARY
FALL OF BATAAN AND CORREGIDOR
ISSUED MAY 7 1944

Quantity 285,000   Scott N35
5-centavos on 20-centavos
ultramarine

Quantity 165,000   Scott N36
12-centavos on 60-centavos
blue-green

Surcharged in black on 20-centavos and 60-centavos
Moro Vinta & Clipper Air Mail stamps of 1941

Issued to commemorate the Second Anniversary of the Fall of Bataan and Corregidor; also contemporaneously called the 'Third Bataan Issue'. The 5-centavos stamp covered the First Class Mail letter rate and the 12-centavos stamp the Registry Fee then in effect.

LAUREL REGULAR ISSUE
ISSUED JANUARY 12 1945

All three values with the same design featuring a portrait of President Jose P Laurel

Imperforate and Ungummed

Quantity 750,000	Quantity 500,000	Quantity 350,000
Scott N37	Scott N38	Scott N39
dull-violet brown	blue-green	chalky-blue

The Laurel Issues formed the last series issued during the Japanese Occupation. They were intended to be issued on the first anniversary of the Republic on October 14 1944 but for some reason this was delayed. Recurrent air raids in Manila disrupted normal activities, and Postal Authorities were only able to sell to the public Imperforate Laurel Issues without gum. A perforated 5-centavos issue of this series is known to exist although never sold to the public.

Lithographed on glazed newsprint, and issued under adverse wartime conditions, the Laurel stamps are crude examples of the printer's art.

SEMI-POSTAL ISSUES

FOOD PRODUCTION CAMPAIGN
ISSUED NOVEMBER 12 1942

Design common to all three values

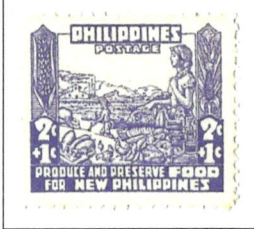  

Quantity 400,000   NB1
2-centavos + 1-centavo
pale violet

Quantity 200,000   NB2
5-centavos + 1-centavo
bright green

Quantity 50,000   NB3
16-centavos + 2-centavos
orange

The extra fees on these stamps, the first semi-postals in Philippine postal history, accrued to the benefit of the Philippine Red Cross. This had been created in 'Executive Order No 31' creating the Philippine Red Cross approved by the Commander-in-Chief of the Imperial Japanese Forces in the Philippines on April 24 1942.

This stamp design had been prepared in late 1941 for two stamps (not semi-postal) to publicise a campaign 'To Produce and Preserve Food for National Defence'. The war intervened, and the revised version in three values 'To Produce and Preserve Food for New Philippines' was issued under the Japanese Administration.

BAHA (FLOOD RELIEF)
ISSUED DECEMBER 8 1943

Surcharged in black on Regular Issue of 1943
Quantity for each stamp value 350,000

Scott NB5	Scott NB6	Scott NB7
12 + 21-centavos	20 + 36-centavos	21 + 40-centavos
steel blue	rose violet	blue violet
Moro Vinta	Nipa Hut	Mayon Volcano & Mt Fuji

These stamps were sold by the Government to provide relief to the victims of the November 1943 Luzon Typhoon which brought much damage to the islands. The stamps surcharged were part of the original issue of 1943 overprinted with the words *baha* (flood) and 1943, the year the flood occurred.

ISSUED 23 JANUARY 1962

Scott E11

Scott E12

POSTAGE DUE

USED BETWEEN SEPTEMBER 3 AND OCTOBER 14 1942

Double bar postage due

USED FROM OCTOBER 13 1942

Single bar postage due

POSTAGE DUE

DOUBLE BAR POSTAGE DUE

USED BETWEEN
SEPTEMBER 1 1942 -
OCTOBER 14 1942

SINGLE BAR POSTAGE DUE

ISSUED OCTOBER 13 1942

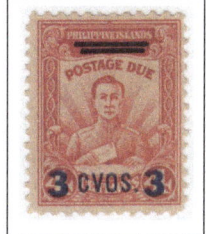

Quantity 1,000   Noted in Scott   Quantity 40,000   Scott NJ1

3-centavos on 4-centavos brown red
Postal Clerk
Overprinted in deep blue on Postage Due Stamp of 1937

Postage due stamps were issued and used in Manila only to cover the deficiency on short paid letters.

Between September 3 1942 and October 14 1942, because of the urgent need for postage due stamps, the words 'United States of America' on 1,000 stamps were blacked out by two hand-ruled bars in India ink. Known as the 'double bar', these stamps were never officially sold and were intended to only be affixed to letters by postal clerks. The double bar stamp has been widely forged. Very few genuine official examples are known to exist.

Japanese Occupation Stamps of the Philippines

ISSUED NOVEMBER 5 2007

Scott 3133a and 3133b
Size is reduced by 20%

OFFICIAL ISSUES

FOR EXCLUSIVE USE OF GOVERNMENT OFFICES
&
GOVERNMENT-CONTROLLED CORPORATIONS

OFFICIAL ISSUE
ISSUED APRIL 7 1943

Quantity 200,000   Scott NO1
Overprinted in black on 2-centavos Regular Issue of 1941
2-centavos apple green
Jose Rizal

The overprinting in kanji characters are *Koyo* or Official Business. K P stands for the Tagalog phrase *Kagamitang Pampamahalaan* (Official Business).

OFFICIAL ISSUE

FIRST OVERPRINTING (MIDDLE BAR LOW)
ISSUED APRIL 7 1943
SECOND OVERPRINTING (MIDDLE BAR HIGH)
ISSUE DATE UNKNOWN

Total quantity for both overprintings 500,000

Both printings known in golden brown and dark brown shades

First Overprinting   Second Overprinting

Scott NO3   Scott NO3a

Golden Brown   Golden Brown

Scott NO3b   Scott NO3c

Dark Brown   Dark Brown

The two overprintings of this stamp are from two separate plates. In the First Overprinting (Middle Bar Low) the distance from the top bar to the middle bar is approximately 10mm; in the Second Overprinting (Middle Bar High) the distance is approximately 8.5mm.

A small number of stamps were overprinted in error on the large Commonwealth stamp Scott 413 (see page 43).

OFFICIAL ISSUE
FIRST OVERPRINTING (MIDDLE BAR HIGH)
ISSUED APRIL 30 1943
SECOND OVERPRINTING (MIDDLE BAR LOW)
ISSUE DATE UNKNOWN
BLOOD COMPACT

First Overprinting   Second Overprinting

Scott NO4   Scott NO4a

Total quantity for both 200,000

Surcharged in black 16-centavos on 30-centavos Regular Issue of 1939

In the First Overprinting, the middle bar is approximately 3.0 to 3.5mm below the top obliterating bar (Middle Bar High). In the Second Overprinting, that distance is approximately 9.0 to 9.5mm (Middle Bar Low).

OFFICIAL ISSUE
OFFICIALLY REPRINTED
ISSUED JUNE 26 1944

Quantity 23,000   Scott NO2
Dark Brown
Surcharged in black 5-centavos on 6-centavos Regular Issue of 1936
La Dalaga (Filipina Maiden)

Early in 1944 it was discovered that among the sheets of then current 5-centavos KP stamps (small Commonwealth) one sheet of large COMMONWEALTH stamps had been wrongly overprinted. It was decided to reproduce and release for sale a limited number of 'replicas' of the original error. These were printed only for the benefit of collectors and not for any postal need.

SECOND OFFICIAL ISSUE
ISSUED AUGUST 28 1944

Total quantity for both 500,000

Scott NO5   Scott NO5a

Golden Brown   Dark Brown

Surcharged in black 5-centavos on 6-centavos Regular Issue of 1936
La Dalaga (Filipina Maiden)

Part of the last series of official issues of the Japanese Administration in the Philippines. Issued after the establishment of the Japanese puppet government, the stamp was surcharged with the words *Republika Ng Pilipinas* and K P, Tagalog for *Kagamitang Pampamahalaan* (Official Business).

SECOND OFFICIAL ISSUE
20-CENTAVOS
ISSUED AUGUST 28 1944

Quantity 200,000   Scott NO6
Overprinted in black on 20-centavos Official Issue of 1940
20-centavos olive bistre
Juan de la Cruz

The 20-centavos Juan de la Cruz stamp was originally released in 1939. Juan de la Cruz symbolized the typical Filipino in Barong Tagalog and salakot hat.

Part of the last series of official issues of the Japanese Administration in the Philippines. Issued after the establishment of the Japanese puppet government, the stamp was surcharged with the words *Republika Ng Pilipinas* and K P, Tagalog for *Kagamitang Pampamahalaan* (Official Business).

SECOND OFFICIAL ISSUE
1 PESO
ISSUED AUGUST 28 1944

Quantity 100,000   Scott NO7
Surcharged in black on 1-peso Air Mail stamp of 1941
1-peso sepia
Moro Vinta & Clipper

Part of the last series of official issues of the Japanese Administration in the Philippines. Issued after the establishment of the Japanese puppet government, the stamp was surcharged with the words *Republika Ng Pilipinas* and K P, Tagalog for *Kagamitang Pampamahalaan* (Official Business).

JAPANESE POSTAL ERA ENDS

American liberation forces landed on Leyte Island on October 20 1944. Nineteen days later, the Post Office of Tacloban was reopened for postal service amidst the still smoking ruins. Pre-war stamps overprinted by hand-stamp with the word VICTORY were available to the public.

However, the Japanese Postal Service did not officially end until February 3 1945, when American Military Forces entered Manila. The Battle for Manila raged for one month until March 4 1945, exactly three years to the day after the commencement of postal services under the Japanese Military Command.

Drawing of Post Office building pre-war

APPENDIX I

OCCUPATION STAMPS ISSUED BEFORE THE WAR

PRE-WAR POSTAL ISSUES

The Japanese Administration selected for use fourteen stamps that were in circulation before the war.

Column 1
Eight stamps had been released under the American Colonial Administration issue of February 15 1935.

Column 2
After the Philippine Commonwealth was created these stamps were overprinted in black with COMMONWEALTH in 1936-37. The overprinted letters were in a heavy type.

Column 3
In 1938-40, overprinting used a slightly smaller type, with the single line overprint measuring 18.5x1.75mm.

Column 1	Column 2	Column 3
No Overprint	Large Commonwealth	Small Commonwealth
Issued February 15 1935	Issued 1936-37	Issued 1938-40

WOMAN & CARABAO

| Scott 384 | Scott 412 | Scott 434 |

LA DALAGA

| Scott 385 | Scott 413 | Scott 435 |

Roderick Hall Collection
Filipinas Heritage Library

PRE-WAR POSTAL ISSUES

Column 1
No Overprint
Issued February 15 1935

Column 2
Large Commonwealth
Issued 1936-37

Column 3
Small Commonwealth
Issued 1938-40

SALT SPRING

Scott 388　　　　　Scott 416　　　　　Scott 438

MAGELLAN LANDING 1521

  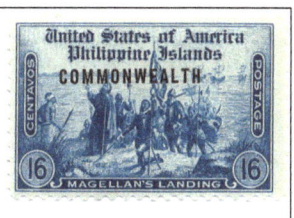

Scott 389　　　　　Scott 417　　　　　Scott 439

JUAN DE LA CRUZ

  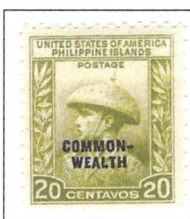

Scott 390　　　　　Scott 418　　　　　Scott 440

Roderick Hall Collection
Filipinas Heritage Library

PRE-WAR POSTAL ISSUES

Column 1
No Overprint
Issued February 15 1935

Column 2
Large Commonwealth
Issued 1936-37

Column 3
Small Commonwealth
Issued 1938-40

BLOOD COMPACT

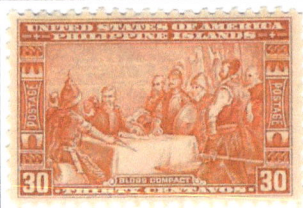 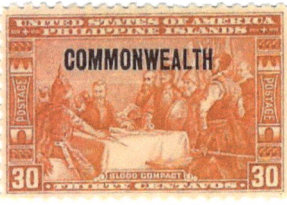 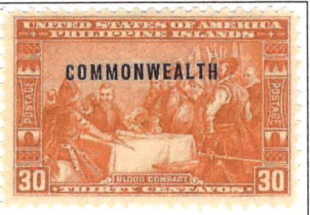

Scott 392   Scott 420   Scott 442

BARASOAIN CHURCH

Scott 393   Scott 421   Scott 443

MONTALBAN GORGE

 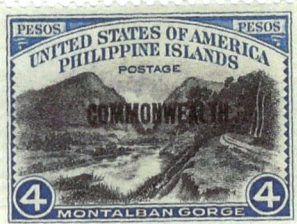 

Scott 395   Scott 423   Scott 445

Roderick Hall Collection
Filipinas Heritage Library

PRE-WAR POSTAL ISSUES

TRANSPACIFIC ISSUE DECEMBER 2 1935

Issued to Commemorate the first China Clipper flight from
Manila to San Francisco
December 2-5 1935

Scott C53

FIRST FOREIGN TRADE WEEK, ISSUE JULY 5 1939

Overprinted in red for first Foreign Trade Week
May 21-27 1939

Scott 449

JOSE RIZAL
Issued April 14 1941

Scott 461

Roderick Hall Collection
Filipinas Heritage Library

PRE-WAR POSTAL ISSUES

The Commonwealth Airmail stamps, Moro Vintage and Clipper, issued on June 30 1941, shown below in their original state, were selected by the Japanese administration for issuance on special occasions.

FIRST ANNIVERSARY
PHILIPPINE EXECUTIVE COMMISSION
January 23 1943

Scott C59   Scott C62

SECOND ANNIVERSARY
FALL OF BATAAN AND CORREGIDOR
May 7 1944

Scott C60   Scott C61

PRE-WAR POSTAGE DUE

On August 21 1928 a series of identical brown-red postage due stamps were issued in seven denominations: 4, 6, 8, 10, 12, 16 and 20-centavos. One of these stamps, the 4-centavos was surcharged in blue with a 3-centavos value on July 29 1937. It is only this surcharged stamp that the Japanese administration selected for use.

Scott J8

Scott J15

PRE-WAR OFFICIAL STAMPS

Column 1	**Column 2**	**Column 3**
Pre-Commonwealth Issued 1935	Issued 1937-38	Issued 1938-40

Scott O16
4-centavos
Woman & Carabao

Scott O28
4-centavos
Woman & Carabao

Scott O17
6-centavos
La Dalaga

Scott O29
6-centavos
La Dalaga

Scott O20
12-centavos
Salt Springs

Scott O3
12-centavos
Salt Springs

Roderick Hall Collection
Filipinas Heritage Library

PRE-WAR OFFICIAL STAMPS

Column 1
Pre-Commonwealth

Column 2
Issued 1937-38

Column 3
Issued 1938-40

Scott O21
16-centavos
Magellan's Landing

Scott O33
16-centavos
Magellan's Landing

Scott O22
20-centavos
Juan de la Cruz

Scott O26
20-centavos
Juan de la Cruz

Scott O34
20-centavos
Juan de la Cruz

Scott O24
30-centavos
Blood Compact

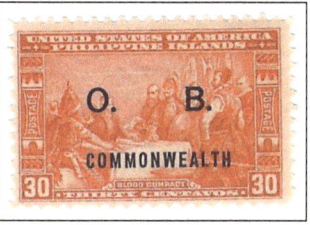

Scott O36
30-centavos
Blood Compact

Japanese Occupation Stamps of the Philippines

OFFICIAL STAMP
ISSUED AUGUST 14 1941

Scott O37
2-centavos
Jose Rizal

Photo of Post Office building in ruins

Roderick Hall Collection
Filipinas Heritage Library

APPENDIX II

LIBERATION
&
VICTORY / COMMONWEALTH

LIBERATION

Original 1944 Philippine invasion plans called for an initial landing at Mindanao on November 15 1944, to secure an Army airfield to cover the Army landings at Leyte. This was to be quickly followed by the second and larger invasion at Leyte on December 20 1944. Thirty days was allowed to complete the Leyte campaign and secure the Provincial capital of Tacloban. Then a Philippine Commonwealth Government could be reinstated and functioning by January 20 1945. An operating civilian postal system would demonstrate traditional governmental services had been restored.

General MacArthur altered the plans: the initial landing was changed to Leyte; the date was advanced to October 20 1944, and Army troops landed with Naval air cover. The Tacloban Post Office opened 18 days later, on November 9 1944, amidst still smoking ruins. Everything was ahead of schedule but the VICTORY COMMONWEALTH stamp issue, that had been printed in Washington DC was still in transit. This was solved by taking locally available stamps and applying the word VICTORY, using a rubber hand stamp and blue ink. The hand stamp broke and was repaired, causing a bend in the word VICTORY. These stamps were used from November 8 1944 until January 18 1945.

Below are the stamps the Japanese Administration had selected for use that were hand-stamped in blue.

POSTAL ISSUES

Quantity 24,400   Scott 464 (on 461)
30-centavos
Jose Rizal

WOMAN & CARABAO

Quantity 807
Scott 465 on 384

LA DALAGA

 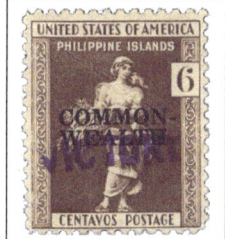

Quantity 64 Quantity 470
Scott 466 on 385 Scott 468 on 413

MAGELLAN'S LANDING

Quantity 122 Quantity 200 Quantity 500
Scott 478 on 389 Scott 479 on 417 Scott 480 on 439

JUAN DE LA CRUZ

Quantity 1,401   Scott 481 on 440

BLOOD COMPACT

Quantity 248   Scott 482 on 420   Quantity 200   Scott 483 on 442

BARASOAIN CHURCH

Quantity 21   Scott 484 on 443

OFFICIAL STAMPS

Quantity 13,100   Scott O39 on O37
Jose Rizal

Quantity 2,634   Scott O40 on O16
Woman & Carabao

Quantity unknown   Scott O40A on O29
La Dalaga

Quantity unknown   Quantity unknown
Scott O42 on O22   Scott O43 on O26
Juan de la Cruz   Juan de la Cruz

VICTORY / COMMONWEALTH

In preparation for the opening of the Tacloban, Leyte Post Office, planned for January 20 1945, a new series of ten stamps was prepared. A two line overprint was used for the first time with a larger VICTORY on the top line and the traditional small COMMONWEALTH overprint on the second line at a new location at the bottom of the stamp. The VICTORY was not an additional overprint, both overprints were simultaneously applied in one operation on all new stamp stocks. The seven stamps below had been used by the Japanese Postal Authorities.

The stamps were printed at the US Bureau of Engraving and Printing in Washington DC between September 28 and October 7 1944. These stamps were still in a convoy crossing the Pacific when the Tacloban Post Office opened on November 8 1944, eighteen days after the invasion. They were first used on January 19 1945, the date originally envisioned before invasion dates were advanced.

Scott 486

4-centavos

Woman & Carabao

yellow green

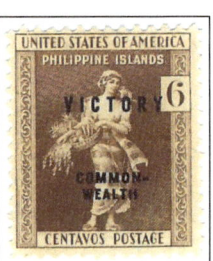

Scott 487

6-centavos

La Dalaga

golden brown

Japanese Occupation Stamps of the Philippines

Scott 490
12-centavos
Salt Spring
black

Scott 491
16-centavos
Magellan's Landing
dark blue

Scott 492
20-centavos
Juan de la Cruz
light olive green

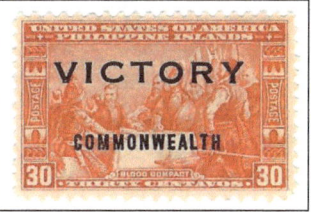

Scott 493
30-centavos
Blood Compact
orange red

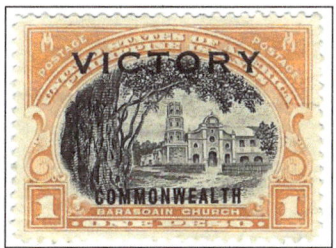

Scott 494
1-peso
Barasoain Church
orange and black

Roderick Hall Collection
Filipinas Heritage Library

Japanese Occupation Stamps of the Philippines

Roderick Hall Collection
Filipinas Heritage Library

Roderick Hall Collection
Filipinas Heritage Library

www.ingramcontent.com/pod-product-compliance
Lightning Source LLC
Chambersburg PA
CBHW042305150426
43197CB00001B/26